Friendship
Fun
Forever

Friendship Fun Forever

by Lori Stacy

SCHOLASTIC INC.
New York Toronto London Auckland Sydney
Mexico City New Delhi Hong Kong

ISBN 0-439-16104-5

Copyright © 2000 by Scholastic Inc.
Published by Scholastic Inc.

SCHOLASTIC and associated logos are trademarks and/or registered trademarks of Scholastic Inc.

12 11 10 9 8 7 6   2 3 4 5/0

Printed in the U.S.A.
First Scholastic printing, February 2000

Special thanks to:
Autumn White and Janet Moore for the crafts and games; Jerry Moore for sharing his magic secrets; Mike Stacy for his sports and business expertise; and especially to Merritt Stokley for all her awesome ideas and input!

Table of Contents

What This Book's All About

Spending time with your friends is lots of fun. With friends around, there's rarely a dull moment. But even the best of pals sometimes need ideas to help them with fun things to do together. That's where this book comes in! It's packed with great ideas for friendship fun: anytime, anyplace, anywhere.

CHAPTER ONE

New Twists on Old Classics

If you're like most kids, you've probably been playing games like tag and hide-and-seek forever! Here are some ideas for making those same games new and even more fun.

TAG

In the game of tag, the object is for the player who's "It" to chase and tag the other players. In these versions, the chase is still on — it's just a little different!

Shadow Tag

Instead of trying to run and tag another player, the person who's It has to step on a player's shadow. If she does, that person becomes the new It. The later in the day you play this version, the longer the shadows become and the harder it is for the players to escape the girl who's It.

Backward Tag

This game's almost exactly like the original tag — except that everyone has to run backward, including the girl who's It. Play this game in a large open area, free of trees or other obstacles, so that no one gets hurt.

Ball Tag

You'll need a rubber ball or an inflatable ball to play. The ball starts off in the hands of one of the players who's not It. The girl who's It can only tag the person carrying the ball. That means that the other players have to keep handing the ball off to one another to avoid being tagged. The next person becomes It if she is tagged while holding the ball or if she drops the ball while it's in play.

Water Balloon Tag

For another twist on ball tag, use a water balloon. Players have to be even more careful when passing the ball in this version, or else they'll wind up getting really wet!

Water Gun Tag

This game is perfect for warm weather days. The person who's It carries a water gun. Instead of trying to tag the other players, she has to shoot the water gun and hit another player.

HIDE-AND-SEEK

In classic hide-and-seek, the person who's It closes her eyes and counts to twenty from "home base" (selected before the game begins) to give the other players a chance to hide. Players hide in an area that's been chosen to be the playing zone. Then it's up to the girl who's It to try and find the hiders before they are able to run and touch home base. Here are a few fun twists on the game for you to try.

Hide-and-seek at Night

Play this game indoors at night in an area that's free from sharp furniture or breakable items. To play, turn off the lights and have the person who's It count to twenty. Instead of running, the players must *crawl* to their hiding places. Once the person who's It is ready to go find the others, she, too, must crawl on her hands and knees and rely only on touch to try to find the other players in the dark. The first person who is tagged then becomes the new It.

Hot and Cold Hide-and-seek

In this version, it's up to the person who's It to hide an object — such as a tennis ball or a pair of socks, while the rest of the players have their eyes closed. When she's finished hiding the object, she calls out, "Ready!" and the other players scramble to try and find the object. The girl who's It helps them along by telling them which players are "cold" (far away from the object) and which players are "hot" (close to the object). If a player who's cold keeps moving farther away from the object, the girl who's It says that player is getting even colder. If, on the other hand, a player who's hot is getting closer to the object, the girl who's It lets her know she's getting even warmer. The first person to find the object becomes It and gets to hide an object next.

RACES

For a race, you need a starting line and a finish line. Check out these fun new ways to challenge players to get from Point A to Point B!

Red Light, Green Light

In this version, select one player to be the stoplight. The stoplight stands at one end of the yard and all the other players stand at the other end. The object is to try and be the first player to reach the stoplight.

The stoplight decides when to let the others approach her by being either a green light (go) or a red light (stop). While she is facing them, she is a red light and all the other players must freeze. Players caught moving while the stoplight's red are sent back to the starting line. When the stoplight turns back around with her back to the other players, she yells, "Green light!" and the players take off toward her. The first player to reach her wins and gets to be the next stoplight.

Three-Legged Race

You'll need teams of two and a bunch of cloth bandanas for this race! Decide on a starting line and a finish line, and have each person select a partner. Have each player stand side by side with her partner, then loosely tie their inside legs together using a cloth bandana. They can put their arms around each other's shoulders to make it easier to run together.

Have all the participants stand ready at the starting line. Choose a "starter" for the games (like a parent) to get things going. When the starter yells, "Go!" the teams take off. The first pair to cross the finish line wins the race.

Wheelbarrow Race

You can use the same twosomes from the three-legged race or select new pairs. Have the pairs line up at the starting line. To get into the wheelbarrow position, one player needs to get down on her hands and knees in front of her teammate. After the starter yells, "Go!" the standing player will need to pick up her teammate's legs by the ankles and hold them at about waist level. It's up to her to "push" the wheelbarrow — her teammate — toward the finish line. Her teammate, as the wheelbarrow, must move forward by walking on her hands.

There are sure to be some spills as players try to make it to the finish line!

Once the players reach the finish line, they have to switch positions and race back. The first team to cross the starting line again wins the race.

Potato Sack Race

This version is called the potato sack race because you'll need burlap potato sacks or old pillowcases for each player participating in the race. Give everyone a sack or a pillowcase and have them line up at the starting line. After the starter yells, "Go!" each girl must step both feet into her sack, hold it up around her body, and hop on two feet to the finish line. If she falls, she can get back up and keep going. The first girl to cross the finish line wins the race!

MOTHER, MAY I?

In "Mother, may I?" the player who's chosen to be "Mother" stands at the finish line and the others line up at the starting line. To move forward, each player takes a turn asking Mother if they may make a specific kind of move forward. For instance, the first player in line may ask, "Mother, may I take two giant steps forward?" It's up to Mother to decide. She either says, "Yes, you may," or she comes up with another answer. For instance, she might say, "No, but you may take two baby steps backward and one giant step forward."

If a player makes a move without getting permission, Mother sends her back to the starting line. The player who reaches Mother first wins the game and gets to be Mother next.

Hot Weather Mother, May I?

If it's hot outside, try playing the game of "Mother, may I?" in the pool! Instead of asking to take giant steps or baby steps, the players ask for permission to take swimming strokes, like backstrokes or dog paddles. And while the players are waiting for their turn, they have to keep treading water!

TUG-OF-WAR

Your friends will have fun testing their strength and coordination in this classic battle. It's traditionally played over a mud puddle, so that the losing team ends up landing in the mud, but this version will keep everyone a little cleaner!

You'll need a long rope with a bandana tied around the center point. Lay the rope out straight on the ground, then mark the center point on the ground with tape or a stick.

Now decide on the two teams. It's best if the teams are equal in strength and size. One way to choose teams is to pick two team captains. Let the team captains pick their players one at a time.

After selecting the teams, each team lines up on either side of the rope. The strongest member of each team should be at the end of the rope. She can tie it loosely around her waist to help anchor it. Everyone else should line up in front of her and grab on to the rope, holding it at waist level.

Once the teams are in position, have the starter yell, "Go!" Both teams then begin pulling the rope, trying to pull the other team across the middle point that you've marked on the ground. Players aren't allowed to cross the center line on the rope, or else the other team automatically wins.

CHAPTER TWO

Great Ideas for When You're Stuck Inside

Just because you can't go outside doesn't mean you can't come up with a ton of fun activities to keep you and your friends busy. Next time you and your pals are looking for a great way to spend the day inside, try one of these ideas.

CHARADES

Charades is a game in which one player acts out a word or phrase while the other players try to guess what it is. The person acting out the phrase can be as silly as she wants while the others are guessing — but she must remain silent.

Here's what you do to start playing charades:

1. Ask someone to come up with all the phrases. (Tip: Have a grown-up come up with the phrases so that you won't have to skip out on guessing.) Some examples of good charades categories are movie titles, book titles, or song titles.

2. Have a grown-up write each phrase or title on a separate sheet of paper.

3. Fold each paper, and place them all together in a bag, a bowl, or a hat.

Here's how to play:

Each player takes a turn choosing a piece of paper from the bag and acting out a specific charade for the other players. Have a stopwatch or timer on hand — each player gets five minutes to play out her charade. The person doing the charade can try to act out the whole title or one word in the title at a time. If the player acting out the phrase speaks, she loses her turn. When a player guesses the correct title, the player acting out the charade nods to let her know she's right. She gets one point if someone guesses the right title, and so does the girl who guessed correctly. The first person to reach five points wins!

Here are some hints to help make the game even more fun:

Type of Title: First, let those players guessing the charade know whether it's a book, movie, or song title.

Clue Them In: Since you must stay silent the whole time, here are clues for those who are guessing. To indicate a song title, wave your hands like a musical conductor. To indicate a movie title, make believe your hands are a video camera by placing them, like a tube, in front of one eye and looking around the room. Finally, for a book title, hold your palms together in front of you, and then fold them open as though you were opening a book. (If the title is both a book and a movie, do both hints.)

Number of Words: Hold up your fingers to show how many words are in the title. Then, if you're going to act out the third word first, hold up three fingers to let the others know. For instance, if you were - trying to get them to guess the book title *Miss Spider's Wedding,* you would hold up three fingers to let them know you were going to be acting out the third word. Then you could pretend to be a bride at a wedding.

The "Sounds Like" Clue: When you're stumped on how to act out a word, think about using the "sounds like" clue — which means the word you're acting out isn't the actual word, but sounds a lot like the actual word. To show you are doing a "sounds like" clue, just tug on your earlobe. For example, take the title from above, *Miss Spider's Wedding.* Sure, it might be easy to act out the word *wedding,* but *miss*?! It would be much simpler to tug on your ear and then pretend to kiss someone. *Kiss* sounds like *miss*. The other players can say all the words that sound like *kiss* until they choose the correct one — *miss*.

IMPROV THEATER

Are you ready to put on a play? Since "improv" (which is short for the word *improvisation*) means making things up on the spot, you won't even need a story to set the stage for this play! All you and your friends will need are good imaginations.

Here's how it works:

Have at least two friends on hand to take part. Create a "stage" for your play by sectioning off an area in one of the bigger rooms in your house. Then place a chair or chairs in front of the stage for the audience to sit on.

Each girl should come up with characters in sticky situations and write them down on three-by-five-inch cards. (You can also have someone who's not playing make a list for all of you to use.) When it's your turn, select one of the cards, and grab a partner or two to help you act out the scene. But don't tell your partner what character and scene you have selected — it's going to be her job to figure out who she's supposed to be!

For instance, say you select a scene about a fisherman whose boat is sinking. You have to pretend you're another character in this situation (for example, a passenger on the boat) and get your friend to figure out who she is and what she should be doing . . . in just two minutes! But you're not allowed to say what's on the card. Instead, you might say something like, "Ahoy, mate! Shall I get you a bucket?" Your friend has to play along, acting with you and trying to get you to give her more clues.

After two minutes is up, it's time to stop acting and see if your audience of friends —

CHARACTER/ SITUATION SUGGESTIONS:

- ◆ **A person who's been sprayed by a skunk**
- ◆ **A taxicab driver who's lost**
- ◆ **A girl who just got braces**
- ◆ **An Olympic ice-skater going for the gold medal**
- ◆ **A scuba diver being chased by a shark**
- ◆ **A bank robber who's just been caught by the police**

or your fellow actor — was able to figure out what was going on. Once you're done, take a bow, then join the audience and let the next pair of girls put on a show for you.

TALENT CONTEST

Show off your stage appeal by holding a talent show among your friends! You will need to find a few friends who want to perform in front of others and a judge or judges who'll be fair, like parents or another friend. You'll also need a "crown" for the winner, which you can create using yellow construction paper.

Give each contest participant a few minutes to come up with a routine. It can be something silly, like singing a funny song or trying to mimic someone famous. Or her talent can be something more serious, like doing a gymnastics stunt or playing the piano.

After the contestants have had a few minutes to practice their routines, bring out the judges! After each girl performs, the judges have to give her a score between one and ten, with ten being the absolute best score. If you use more than one judge, you can add up all the judges' scores for a final tally. After all the contestants have performed, one of the judges presents the "crown" to the girl with the highest score.

PLAYING DRESS-UP

To play dress-up, first come up with a theme. You might pick something like "circus" or "the Wild West," or select a time period, such as the 1950s or the 1970s.

Then you and your friends dress up according to the theme. Don't forget to fix your hair, or add accessories and jewelry to complete your costume. After each girl comes up with a costume, it's time for all of you to model the costumes for a grown-up or another person who can serve as judge. She can judge your costumes on originality, accuracy, or anything else you decide.

Once you're done, come up with another theme and start again!

MAKING MAGIC

Show your friends that you have a few tricks up your sleeve by putting on a magic show. You can find simple magic-trick kits at toy and hobby stores. Or have fun doing these easy tricks for your friends.

CANDY MAGIC

Bet you didn't know that eating a Life Savers candy could create some sparks. It's true — the sugar crystals in Wint-O-Green Life Savers create a charge that's visible in the dark when you chew them. All you will need to try this simple experiment is a few Wint-O-Green Life Savers, a friend, and a really dark place, like a closet or a bathroom without windows. Shut yourself in the dark area and wait a few minutes until your eyes adjust to the darkness. After your eyes have adjusted, crunch the Life Savers for your friend to see. Forget your manners for this trick — you'll need to chomp on the Life Savers with your mouth open so that your friend can see the Wint-O-Green Life Savers light up the dark with their tiny, lightning-bolt-like charges. Then have your friend do the crunching so that you watch the sparks fly, too.

The Thumb Trick

With this trick you pretend to remove your thumb from your hand and give it to someone else.

What you need:
- *A handkerchief*
- *A baby carrot or carrot stick as thick as your thumb*

What you do:

1. With your back to your friends (so they can't see what you're doing) hide the carrot in your left hand. Make a fist so no one can see the carrot.

2. Hold up your right-hand thumb and show your friends, then ask a friend to cover your right hand with the handkerchief.

3. With your right hand covered by the handkerchief, place your left hand under the carrot where your thumb is supposed to be.

4. Have the same friend hold on to the thumb (the carrot). Then pull your hand

away — she'll still be holding on to the "thumb."

The Sugar Cube Trick

Amaze your friends with a "magical" sugar cube!

What you need:
- *A sugar cube*
- *A glass of water*
- *A felt-tip pen*

What you do:

1. Ask a friend to write a number between 1 and 10 on one side of the sugar cube.

2. Without looking at the number she has written, place the cube between your thumb and forefinger so that your thumb is pressing the side she wrote on.

3. Press firmly on the cube with your finger and thumb. Then drop the cube into the glass of water.

4. While the sugar cube is dissolving, have your friend place her hand in yours.

5. Press the thumb that held the sugar cube onto her palm. (This will transfer the number from your thumb to her palm.)

6. Hold her hand above the glass, "commanding" the dissolved sugar cube to reveal the number.

7. Turn her palm over to reveal the number she selected and wrote down.

CREATE A TIME CAPSULE

Wouldn't it be nice to hang on to special memories you've shared with friends? Create a friendship time capsule — a box containing memories from today that you and your friends promise not to open again until a later date.

What you need:
- *Shoe box*
- *Construction paper*
- *Scissors*
- *Glue or tape*

What you do:

1. Decorate the shoe box by covering it with colorful construction paper. Add any other decorations you want, like stickers, stamps, or pictures.

2. Then it is time for you and your friends to fill the box with predictions for the future and items that hold meaning for all of you (but that you won't mind living without for a while!).

ITEMS YOU MAY WANT TO PLACE IN YOUR TIME CAPSULE

◆ Pictures of you and your friends.

◆ A note from each girl about what's happening in her life at the moment — who her best friends are, how she spends her time, her favorite celebrity, her favorite class, etc.

◆ Wishes for the future — what you hope will happen between the time when you bury the time capsule and when you dig it up.

Once you've filled the box with favorite memories and future predictions, seal it with sturdy tape and write on it, "Do not open until ___." (Come up with a future date to open the time capsule, like six months from now or a year from now. . . . The longer you can wait, the more fun it will be to open the box and recall those memories.)

Put the time capsule away somewhere that makes it easy to forget about it for a while. . . . It might be too hard to resist opening it if it's right there on your dresser! Then make a promise with your pals that, if at all possible, you'll get together in the future on the date you've noted to open the time capsule and look at the contents.

BAKE-FEST

Crummy weather is the best weather for holing up in the kitchen with a friend to bake something yummy. What are you in the mood to make? Look through recipe books for ideas, or try one of the recipes here. Whatever you decide to bake, keep in mind these cooking tips:

- *Before you begin baking, check to make sure you have all of the ingredients that you'll need, along with a grown-up's permission and help.*
- *Be sure everybody involved has clean hands, and if you have long hair, you may want to tie it back in a ponytail so that it doesn't get in your way . . . or in your food!*
- *Be oven-safe. Don't put your face too near the open oven, and be sure to use pot holders or an oven mitt to remove food from the oven — or have a grown-up do this part for you. Don't forget to turn off the oven when you are done baking.*
- *Use care when handling knives or other sharp objects. Again, it's best to have a grown-up's help.*
- *If you are using the stovetop, don't leave metal spoons or instruments in the pan while you are cooking. Their handles will get extremely hot. Remember, too, that stovetops stay*

hot even after you turn them off (especially electric stoves).

- *Tempting as it may be, try not to taste what you've made until it has cooled . . . otherwise, you might end up with a sore tongue!*

Recipes

Peanut Butter Balls

What you need:
- *1 cup peanut butter (creamy or chunky)*
- *1 cup powdered sugar*
- *½ cup milk*
- *1 teaspoon vanilla extract*
- *2 cups quick oats*
- *Optional: 1 cup of chocolate chips, miniature marshmallows, or raisins, or a 1 cup mixture of all three*
- *Large bowl*
- *Large mixing spoon*
- *Measuring cups*
- *Measuring spoons*

- *Waxed paper*
- *Large tray or plate*

What you do:

1. Mix together peanut butter, sugar, milk, and vanilla in a large bowl.

2. Add oats and extra ingredients, if using, and stir until mixed well.

3. Form balls the size of large marbles, then place on a waxed-paper-lined plate or tray.

4. Refrigerate the balls for one hour. To keep, store in an airtight container.

Makes approximately 36 balls.

Choose-a-Chip Cookies

What you need:
- *¾ cup sugar*
- *¾ cup brown sugar*
- *2 eggs*
- *1 teaspoon vanilla extract*
- *1 cup butter or margarine (softened)*
- *2¾ cups all-purpose flour*

- *1 teaspoon baking soda*
- *2 cups baking chips of your choice (such as semisweet chocolate chips, milk chocolate chips, white chocolate chips, or butterscotch chips)*
- *Large mixing bowl*
- *Large spoon*
- *Measuring cups*
- *Measuring spoons*
- *Cookie sheet*

What you do:

1. Preheat the oven to 350°F.

2. Mix together sugars, eggs, vanilla, and butter until creamy and smooth.

3. Add flour and baking soda and stir until blended.

4. Add chips and mix in evenly.

5. Drop rounded teaspoonfuls of dough 2 inches apart onto cookie sheet.

6. Bake for 7–8 minutes, or until cookies are lightly browned. Carefully remove

from the oven and let cool for 2 minutes on the cookie sheet.

Makes approximately 48 cookies.

Ice-Cream Cone Cupcakes

What you need:
- *1 package cake mix of your choice, plus extra ingredients/utensils needed to make the cake (listed on box)*
- *24 flat-bottomed ice-cream cones*
- *1 jar frosting*
- *Baking sheet*
- *Mixing bowl*
- *Measuring cups*
- *Optional: candy sprinkles or other cake-decorating candies*

What you do:

1. Preheat oven to the temperature listed on the cake mix box.

2. Prepare cake batter according to directions on the box.

3. Fill each ice-cream cone three-quarters full (about one-half inch from top) with cake batter and place filled cones on baking sheet.

4. Place baking sheet in oven and bake according to the cake mix directions. To check if cupcakes are done, insert a toothpick into the middle of one. If it comes out clean (without batter on it), cupcakes are done. Carefully remove from oven and let cool for at least a half hour.

5. Spread icing over top of each cupcake. If you want, you can decorate them with candy sprinkles.

Makes 24 cupcakes.

CARD GAMES

You'd be amazed at how many games you can play with just a deck of cards. These easy games are great for two or more players.

Concentration

Concentration is a game that tests your memory against your opponent's. Shuffle the cards and then lay them all spread out and facedown on the floor. One at a time each player tries to turn over two similar number cards (or two of the same royal cards, for example two queens). They don't need to be the same color or the same suit (such as hearts or spades). They just need to have the same number. If a player gets a pair, she gets to keep the cards and take another turn. When all the cards have been matched, whoever has the most cards in her pile wins.

Go Fish

Deal up a game your friends are sure to love — hook, line, and sinker!

Shuffle the cards and then deal seven cards to each player. Place the rest of the deck facedown in a pile in the center of the table. Each girl should look through her hand of cards to see if she has any pairs (two of the same-numbered cards). If she does, she should lay the pair faceup on the table. Next, it's time to go "fishing" for other pairs!

The girl to the left of the dealer goes first by asking any other player for a card that she needs to make a match. She does this by saying, "Alexa, do you have a four?" for instance. If the player she asks has that card, the player has to give it to her and the starting player gets to continue to play. If not, the other player replies by saying, "Nope. Go fish!" The starting player must then draw a card from the pile and end her turn unless she gets the card she was asking for from the pile. If this happens, she gets to put that pair faceup on the table and draw another card. After all the cards have been paired, the game is over. Count the number of pairs each person has. The girl with the most pairs is the winner.

War

In this card game for two, you and an opponent try to win cards from each other.

Shuffle the cards. Deal all the cards so you each have the same number and there are none left. To begin the game, each of you should take the first card on your pile and place it faceup in the center of the table at the same time. Whoever has the higher-ranking card gets to keep both cards and place them in a second pile off to the side — her winnings pile. The higher the number, the better the card ranks. Face cards, like jacks, are higher than numbered cards, and go in order from lowest ranking to highest ranking: jack, queen, king, ace.

Keep repeating this process until you have gone through your piles. If you happen to place the same card down, then you go to "war" to see who wins the pile. Each of you must place three cards facedown next to your original card and then, at the same time, place the fourth card faceup

THE TEN BEST BOARD GAMES

Not in the mood to use your brainpower to come up with clever games? Then try one of these tried-and-true board games:

- ◆ **Pictionary Junior**
- ◆ **Clue**
- ◆ **Trivial Pursuit Junior**
- ◆ **Sorry!**
- ◆ **Girl Talk**
- ◆ **Checkers**
- ◆ **Outburst Junior**
- ◆ **Mall Madness**
- ◆ **Monopoly Junior**
- ◆ **Scattergories Junior**

on the table. The whole pile of cards goes to the girl whose fourth card is higher-ranking. (And if you have another tie, you have to go to war again!)

Once you've gone through the pile of cards you were dealt, count the number of cards that you have in your pile of winnings. The girl with the most cards wins.

CHAPTER THREE

Snow What?!

Don't get "cabin fever" by staying inside all the time while there's snow on the ground. Instead, take a break by putting on some warm clothes and heading outside for fun in the snow with your friends!

SNOW FORTS

Create an outdoor fort out of snow. All you'll need is an area where there's lots of snow to use, and a pair of warm gloves or mittens to keep your hands from getting too cold. You can also use a snow shovel to help in your snow-gathering efforts.

Build the four walls of your fort by shaping big blocks of snow — and make sure the bases (the bottoms) of the blocks are larger than the tops. Otherwise, the snow might topple over. Leave an opening in the back wall of your fort so that you can get in and out. Build the walls of the fort as high as you like. You can even create decorative corners: Just pack a small plastic pail with snow and then place it upside down on the top of each of the four corners of your fort. Once you're done making your fort, you'll be prepared to protect yourself from flying snowballs!

SNOW MAZES

One of the great things about the ground being covered with snow is that you can track footprints — which makes creating a snow maze supereasy.

Have your friends wait inside while you make the maze. Create a starting point in the snow (try writing the word *start* in the snow), and then decide on a finishing point, such as a tree. Now start walking in the snow in a pattern that will eventually reach the tree, but don't head directly there. Instead, make some turns that lead to nowhere — by walking a few steps in one direction, then going backward, stepping inside your own footprints. You can make it as complicated as you want, creating tons of turnoffs that lead to obstacles or to nowhere. When you're finished with the turnoffs, complete the path to the tree. Finally, have your friends come out and try to follow the right path to get to the finishing point.

SNOWBALL-THROWING CONTEST

Here's a new twist on snowball fights that will keep you and your friends out of the line of fire. You'll need to find a few items to serve as targets, such as large pails, a trash can, or even hula hoops. Of course, you'll also need a good supply of snowballs. Pack them tightly so they won't fall apart as you throw them.

To play, find an area to shoot from. You can mark a line with a stick to make sure that everyone knows where it is. Then set out your targets in front of the line. Place one fairly close to the line, and position the others farther back. Assign points for each target — the farther back it is, the more points it'll be worth if you get it in the target.

Take turns trying to throw a snowball at a target. Come up with the total amount of points needed to win. The first player to reach that number wins.

PAINTED SNOW ANGELS

Practically anyone who's been in the snow knows how to make a snow angel. But with a little food coloring, you can make snow angels that are sensational! All you will need are clean plastic squirt bottles and food coloring. Fill each bottle with water and then add a few drops of food coloring. Place the top back on the bottle, and shake gently to mix. Use a different color for each bottle.

Once you're outside, make your snow angels by lying on the ground on your back with your hands next to your sides. Move your hands up to shoulder-height, still holding them in the snow, to create the angel's wings. Move your legs apart in the snow to create the angel's gown. Pull yourself up carefully to reveal the snow angel.

Now it's time to decorate her! Use the food coloring in the bottles to paint your snow angels. You can spray on a halo, add color where her hair would be, and paint her wings and gown. You and your friends can try to create angels that look like you by using the colors that match your hair and eyes. Be sure to get a picture, because one good snowfall — or one warm day — will take away your angel for good!

SNOW ICE CREAM

Fresh, clean, new-fallen snow makes a great wintertime treat!

What you need:

- ½ cup milk or cream
- ¼ cup sugar
- ¼ teaspoon vanilla extract
- Lots of fresh, clean new snow
- Large bowl
- Small bowl
- Spoon or wire whisk
- Mixing cups
- Measuring spoons
- Spoon for each girl

What you do:

1. Start inside first. Mix together milk, sugar, and vanilla in the small mixing bowl using a wire whisk or spoon. Try to dissolve the sugar in the milk mixture.

2. Go outside with the large bowl and fill it with clean snow. Bring it inside and pour the milk mixture over the snow. Stir gently to mix the milk mixture evenly in the snow. If the mixture is too runny, add more snow until the consistency is like ice cream.

3. Dig in with your spoons and enjoy!

HIGH-STYLE SNOWPEOPLE

Why not give ordinary snowmen and snowwomen makeovers?! With some old clothes and accessories, you can come up with clever new ways to get Frosty and friends looking their best.

First you and your buds will need to do a search for old clothes and accessories, as well as dream up creative ideas for making your snowpeople. Look through your old dress-up clothes, or ask Mom and Dad for items they don't mind letting you use. Think of themes for your snow creations. Here's a list of some to try:

- *A ballerina snowgirl: Find an old tutu to tie around her waist.*
- *A princess snowgirl: Add a toy crown and a glamorous gown.*
- *The movie star: Put a big, floppy hat and dark glasses on her, then add a feather boa and lots of beaded necklaces.*
- *The sporty snowman: Add a baseball*

cap and an old uniform. Use sticks for arms, and add an old glove to one.

When making your snowpeople, be sure to make them a little smaller than normal so the old clothes will fit on them.

When you use your imagination, you'll find that the ideas are endless! See who can come up with the most creative snow-person design, or work together to create a snow work of art!

CHAPTER FOUR

Too Hot to Handle

How can you bear playing outdoors when it's sizzling hot? It's simple: Just add water. Water games are a great way to beat the heat. Stay cool with these really wet ideas!

WATER BALLOON TOSS

You should have enough balloons for each pair of girls to have one (and you might even want to have extras just in case they break too soon). Fill balloons up with water. Careful: The more water you put in each balloon, the more easily it will pop. Give each pair of girls a water balloon. Players should stand face-to-face with their partners, about three big steps apart. On the count of three, the girl holding the balloon tosses it to her partner.

Next have each girl take a step backward. Count to three again and have the girls throw the balloons back to their partners. It's more difficult this time. Teams that drop and break their balloon are out of the game — and probably wet.

TWISTS ON THE WATER BALLOON TOSS

Wedding Bouquet Toss: Stand with your back facing your friends and toss the balloon behind you to see who can catch it.

Water Balloon Fight: The object of this version is just to get everyone else wet while you stay dry.

Hide the Balloon: One person hides the water balloon and the others try to find it. Whoever finds the balloon must throw it at another player and get her wet in order to win the round.

The remaining teams should take another step back and toss the balloons again. The winning team keeps its balloon alive the longest and stays dry.

POOL FUN

When you really need relief from the heat, there's no better place to be than in a pool. Here are a few ideas for pool-time fun with your pals. Be sure that you are a very good swimmer to play these games.

T-Shirt Relays

You'll need to have at least four girls to play this game, as well as a few T-shirts you won't mind having in the pool. Select teams consisting of two girls each, and then have the first girl on each team put on a T-shirt over her swimsuit. The second girl on the team should wait at the opposite end of the pool. Have someone yell, "Go!" and the race begins.

The first girls must swim to the other end, then take off the T-shirts and give them to their teammates. Then it's up to the teammates to put on the T-shirts and swim back to the starting line. The team that finishes first wins.

Capture the Watermelon

For this game, you'll need a watermelon that's not too heavy and a tub of petroleum jelly (such as Vaseline). Rub the outside of the watermelon with petroleum jelly, then place it on the bottom of the pool near the shallow end. Beware: The watermelon will be mighty hard to hold on to! When you and your friends are ready, jump into the pool and see who can get the superslippery watermelon out of the pool first.

Underwater Tea Party

Don't worry — you won't need to bring your mom's favorite teacups into the pool with you for this party. The only thing you'll be holding underwater is your breath!

Go underwater with your friends and begin your "tea party" by pretending to pour each of your pals a cup of tea. Once the make-believe tea has been served, pretend to pick up your cups and sip your tea. See how long you can stay underwater before you either lose your breath or float to the top. Keep on trying until you're able to create the perfect tea party underwater.

Marble Pickup

Remember those little blowup pools you played in when you were very young? Well, you can still have fun in one now that you're older! Here's how:

What you need:
- *Small inflatable pool*
- *Marbles*
- *Small pail or bucket for each girl*

What you do:

1. Blow up the pool and fill it with water.
2. Drop the marbles into the pool.

3. Have everyone sit around the pool with just their feet in it and their buckets next to them. The object of the game is to get as many marbles as you can from the bottom of the pool into your bucket, using only your feet and toes to get them out. The girl who collects the most marbles in her bucket wins.

CHAPTER FIVE

Getting Sporty

Let the athlete in you shine by playing these sports activities with your friends.

BASKETBALL: H-O-R-S-E

If you have access to a basketball and a basketball hoop, then you can play the game of horse.

Before you start to play, decide your lineup by selecting who goes first and in what order the others will follow. The first person then selects a spot anywhere in front of the hoop and tries to shoot the ball into the basket. She can do it underhand, overhand, or even standing backward. If she makes it, each player in line behind her must attempt to make the shot from the same spot and in the same way. If a player fails, she gets the letter *H*.

After everyone has a turn, the first player gets to go again and must come up with another shot for the others to try. If she misses her shot, the second player gets to start and the first player goes to the end of the line. The second player then picks a spot to shoot from (and if she misses, the third player tries, then the fourth, and so on, until one makes it). Any time a player misses a shot, she gets a letter, in order, from the word *horse*.

Once a girl loses enough shots to spell *horse,* she's out of the game. Play continues until there's only one player left — the winner!

SOCCER: CRAB SOCCER

This game of soccer looks a little silly, which makes it even more fun to play! All you'll need is a grassy area (that's free of trees) and a soccer ball. You'll also need a way to create the goalposts, such as marking off an area on each side of the field with stones, sticks, or other objects. Decide beforehand which areas are out-of-bounds.

Choose players for the two teams. Place the ball in the center of the field between the players. Get in the "crab" position: Each player must lie on her back and bend her knees to the ground, then prop herself up with her hands. Everyone must move like a crab with their hands and feet during the whole game. Have someone yell, "Go!" Each team then tries to get the ball in the opponent's goal by using only their feet to move the ball forward.

Select a number of points that a team must get in order to win, and play until the first team reaches that number.

SOFTBALL: PICKLE

You and two friends can see how well you dodge between two bases by playing the game of pickle. You'll need two softball gloves and a softball, as well as items to use as bases, such as two old pillowcases or doormats.

To play, first set up your two bases about the length of a school bus apart (or a shorter distance depending on what you're comfortable with). Decide what's out-of-bounds, so that a person running from base to base can't stray too far away. Select two players to be the fielders: They stand on the bases with the gloves and the ball. The third player, the runner, will try to run from one base to the other without being caught. The runner starts on the base opposite the girl who's holding the ball. The two fielders then toss the ball back and forth to each other.

Whenever she's ready, the runner can start to run from the base she's standing on to the other. She might want to wait until one fielder misses the ball to get a good head start. If she gets caught in the middle, the "pickle" begins. The fielder holding the ball must try to tag the runner out or throw the ball to the other fielder to prevent the runner from reaching her base. When the runner is finally tagged out, she becomes a fielder and switches places with the girl who tagged her out.

IN-LINE SKATING: OBSTACLE COURSE

If you love to in-line skate (otherwise called "Rollerblading"), you'll love the extra challenge involved when you and your friends come up with "obstacles" to avoid. You'll need a large paved area to skate in that's free from cars or other dangers. You'll also need different-colored chalk to draw on the ground. And of course, you'll need the protective gear you normally wear when you skate, including a helmet, knee guards, elbow guards, and wrist guards.

Decide first what the different colors of chalk mean. Pick blue, for instance, to show the boundaries of the course, or the lines you must be within to stay in the game. Be sure the lines are far enough apart so you have room to skate.

You can draw circles of red that must be avoided by either skating around them or jumping over them. Finally, you can block off sections in yellow, which indicate areas that you must skate over on one foot or squatted down.

For an added challenge, you can even place a ball within the boundaries that you must try to pick up while completing the course. Don't forget to mark a start and finish point on your obstacle course!

Once you're done creating the course, take turns trying to complete it by staying inbounds, avoiding the "obstacles," and following the other rules of the course. See who can get through the course first without making a mistake!

VOLLEYBALL: MONKEY IN THE MIDDLE

You and two friends can play this game with a football or another large, soft ball.

To start, select a player to be in the middle. The other two players stand about two body-lengths apart and begin throwing the ball back and forth to each other. The object of the game is for the girl in the middle to intercept the ball by getting it away from the other two — without touching them. To keep her from doing this, the other two can throw the ball high in the air to each other. They also need to be sure and catch the ball; otherwise the girl in the middle can intercept it by getting to it first.

Whoever doesn't catch the ball and lets it get away must then go in the middle and try to intercept the ball from the other two players.

BEING A GOOD SPORT

For almost every game, there's going to be a winner and a loser. And while victory can be thrilling, defeat can make you feel pretty bad. But nothing is worse than a sore loser (except maybe a sore winner!). That's why it's important to show good sportsmanship. Here are some tips for losing like a real winner:

◆ Congratulate the winner or winners and say, "Good game." Show them that you aren't holding a grudge because you lost!

◆ Focus not only on what you did right during the game, but also what things you might want to try doing differently in the next game. How can you improve your skills?

◆ If the winners are bragging about their victory, don't get upset. The best way to stop the boasting is by not paying any attention to it.

◆ If you suspect a cheater, say something during the game. Making an issue out of it after the fact might make it seem like you're a sore loser.

◆ Remember why you were playing the game in the first place — to have a good time! As long as you're having fun and trying hard, it shouldn't matter whether or not you're knocking the socks off your opponent!

CHAPTER SIX

Getting Creative

Craft activities are great for you to do alone or together with friends. Let the artist in you shine with these fun, easy crafts!

FRIENDSHIP BRACELETS

What better way to celebrate your friendship than by making each other friendship bracelets? With a few twists and knots, you can come up with tons of great designs. Here's one to get you started:

Knotted Bracelet

You'll need three strands of colored thread, each about twenty-four inches long. Knot the threads together at one end, and then tape the knotted end to the top of a table.

Pull the threads apart from one another, and keep them straight and flat. Then take the first thread on the left (#1) and knot it onto the thread to the right of it (#2). Then, knot thread #1 to #3. After you've finished that row, start knotting #2 onto #3, then to #1. Keep going until the bracelet is long enough to go around your friend's wrist. Trim the ends, making sure to leave enough room so that she can tie it around her wrist.

FUN WITH BEADS

With an assortment of beads and a few other items you're sure to find around the house, you can make colorful, cool jewelry and other accessories. Beads are also easy to find at craft or hobby stores, some toy stores, or discount department stores. To keep your bead collection organized, use a plastic container with compartments, such as a sewing box or fishing tackle box. In it, you'll want not only your beads, but also things like a pair of scissors, colorful embroidery threads, twine, buttons, shoelaces, eraser heads, safety pins, and leather strings. Here are a few items you can make with beads:

Safety Pin Charm

Thread a row of beads onto a medium- or large-size safety pin. You can secure them in place with a small eraser head. Wear the decorated safety pins on your shirt, jacket, or hat, or fasten one or more to your backpack.

Bracelets and Necklaces

Use either twine, leather strings, or embroidery thread as the base for your bead bracelet or necklace. Fasten one end by tying a knot that's bigger than the hole of the end bead (so it won't slip off). Thread beads onto your base. You can separate each with a knot, add knots in various sections, or simply keep adding beads. Once you have finished, tie another knot to secure the opposite end. Tie loosely around your wrist or neck.

Decorative Shoelaces

Make your shoes stand out by adding colorful beads to the shoelaces. Remove your shoelaces from your shoes. Add a few beads to one shoelace, and position them in the center of it. Thread the shoelace into the last two holes (nearest your toes) so that the beads in the middle are on top. Continue rethreading your shoelaces, adding beads along the way. Once you have threaded your shoelaces, you can add a bead to the end of each lace by tying a knot above and below the bead.

MAKING PLAY CLAY

Colored clay is easy to make and requires ingredients you probably already have at home. Once you make the clay, you can use it to create shapes and objects.

What you need:
- *1 cup flour*
- *1 cup water*
- *½ cup salt*
- *1 tablespoon cooking oil*
- *2 tablespoons cream of tartar*
- *Food coloring (any color you like)*
- *A large saucepan*
- *A large wooden spoon*
- *Plastic container to store the clay*
- *A grown-up to help you*

CLAY-SHAPES GAME

Use your home-made clay for a game that's similar to the popular board game Pictionary. Instead of drawing your clues for your teammates, you shape the clay to look like the clue you're given!

What you do:

1. Place all the ingredients except the food coloring in the saucepan. Then add a few drops of food coloring and mix well.

2. Set the saucepan on the stove over medium heat. Stir constantly until

the mixture forms into clay.

3. Let the clay cool down in the saucepan before you transfer it to a plastic container. You can keep it stored in its sealed container inside the refrigerator for up to two weeks.

DECORATIVE PENCIL CUPS

Make pretty pencil cups using paint and jars. Try using glass jelly jars, or other food jars that your pencils and pens will fit into nicely. Be sure you're wearing clothes that you won't mind getting a little paint on, or wear an apron or smock.

What you need:
- *A clean, empty glass jar for each girl (to make it easy to remove labels that are pasted on, soak the jars in warm water for a few minutes)*
- *Paint (either acrylic or liquid tempera paints will work)*

- *White glue*
- *Small paper or plastic cups*
- *Newspaper*
- *Paintbrushes*
- *Ribbon*
- *Optional: clear craft glaze*

What you do:

1. Spread newspaper out on the table where you'll be working.

2. In a cup, mix each color of paint with a little glue. Then paint designs on the outside of the jar. Let the paint dry for at least an hour.

3. If you wish, use the clear glaze to keep the paint from chipping off the glass too easily.

4. Finish off your pencil cup by tying a ribbon around the rim of the jar.

5. Then fill it with pencils, pens, scissors, or other supplies. Or give it to someone as a gift — like your teacher!

PINECONE BIRD FEEDER

This craft will make the birds in the neighborhood happy!

What you need:
- *Pinecones*
- *Sturdy string*
- *Peanut butter*
- *Birdseed*
- *A plastic knife*
- *A paper plate*

What you do:

1. Fasten the string around the top of the pinecones and tie securely.

2. Use the plastic knife to spread peanut butter over the pinecones.

3. Spread about a cup of birdseed on a plate, then, one at a time, roll the pinecones in so they are completely covered.

4. Hang the feeder in a tree or on the patio, and watch for birds to stop in for a meal!

BEING A FRIEND BY YOURSELF

Like it or not, there are going to be times when it's just not possible to be with your friends. But that doesn't mean you have to stop being a friend! Here are some ways you can celebrate your friendships even when your friends aren't around:

◆ Write a special poem for your best friend.

◆ Watch a TV show together by phone. . . . Call her up at commercial breaks and try to guess what's going to happen next.

◆ Bake a treat for your buds and bring it to them at school the next day.

◆ Make a friendship bracelet (see page 60).

◆ Create a friendship collage. Cut out words and letters from magazine ads and articles to form sayings about your friendship, like "Best Friend" or "Keeps Secrets" or "Soccer Star."

◆ Chat on-line with friends. Create a private chat room for your pals and share your thoughts on-line. (Try America Online or Talk City to find areas for private chats.)

◆ If it's the season, make holiday-time crafts like these for all of your friends:

HOLIDAY CRAFTS

Depending on what time of year it is, you can create holiday-themed crafts like these.

Valentine's Day Card Boxes

Store your special valentines in a decorative "mailbox."

What you need:
• *A shoe box*

- *Red, pink, or white felt and/or colored paper*
- *Scissors*
- *Glue*
- *Items to decorate your box with (like buttons, glitter, ribbon, and sequins)*

What you do:

1. Cut a slit in the center of the top of the shoe box that's about a half inch deep and five inches long. Be careful when doing this — you might even want to have your parents cut the slits out of your boxes for you.

2. Cut out sheets of felt or colored paper that are the same size as the top and the sides of the shoe box. You can create an outline that will be easy to cut out by placing the shoe box on top of the felt or paper and tracing around it. Be sure to make a slit in the section of felt or paper you cover the top of the box with.

3. Glue the colored felt or paper to the box. You can then decorate the sides by

gluing on colorful buttons, heart-shaped felt cutouts, glitter, or ribbon.

4. Use your box to collect and store your Valentine's Day cards.

Confetti-Filled Easter Eggs

You'll have a blast cracking these eggs over your friends' heads!

What you need:
- *Eggs (uncooked)*
- *Easter egg dye*
- *Cups or mugs to mix the dye in*
- *Colorful confetti (you can make this with scraps of construction paper or tissue paper)*
- *A straight or safety pin*
- *Tape*

What you do:

1. Carefully poke a hole the size of a dime in the bottom of an egg using the pin. Then turn the egg back up over a bowl to remove the yolk. (Hint: If you don't want

the yolks to go to waste, use the eggs for cooking or baking.)

2. Gently rinse the eggs out with warm running water. Let them air-dry on a towel overnight, or until they are completely dry.

3. Prepare the Easter egg dye according to package directions, then carefully color each of the eggs in the dye. Let them dry completely.

4. When they are dry, fill with confetti.

5. Seal the hole with tape.

6. Now you're ready to crack your egg over the head of an unsuspecting friend!

Fall Leaf Press

Welcome autumn with an easy-to-do leaf press.

What you need:
- *Leaves*
- *Waxed paper*
- *Towel*
- *Iron*

- A *grown-up to help you*

What you do:

1. First gather fallen leaves. Look for leaves in different shapes, sizes, and colors. Make sure that the leaves aren't *too* dried out — otherwise they will crack and fall apart!

2. Place an assortment of leaves between two sheets of waxed paper.

3. Place them on an ironing board and cover with a towel.

4. Then have your mom or another adult iron over them with an iron that's set on low. You'll wind up with a colorful, decorative leaf mosaic that you can frame and/or hang.

Halloween Scarecrows

These cute little scarecrows make perfect Halloween decorations!

What you need:
- *Small and medium brown paper bags*

- *Newspaper*
- *Colored construction paper*
- *Markers and/or crayons*
- *Tape*
- *Scissors*
- *Optional: raffia or string*

What you do:

Make the Scarecrow

1. Stuff a medium-size bag with crumpled newspaper.

2. Fold the two sides of the bag in three inches toward the center and tape them down.

3. Fold the top over about an inch and tape it down. Turn the bag over.

4. Fill a small bag halfway with crumpled newspaper.

5. Twist the top of the bag and then use tape or string to fasten it shut.

6. Cut a small hole in the top of the body and insert the twisted section of the head into the hole so that only the head is

sticking out. Tape it into place.

Finish Your Scarecrow

1. Use your scissors and either brown colored paper or a paper bag to cut out arms and legs.

2. Attach them to the body.

3. Use raffia or string for the "hay." Glue the hay around the scarecrow's neck, and at his wrists and ankles. You can also use the raffia for his hair.

4. Decorate the scarecrow using the markers, crayons, or construction paper. Create his face and funny clothes for his body (like overalls).

5. Set him on a table or on the front porch to greet your trick-or-treaters.

Homemade Christmas Ornaments

These ornaments will look almost good enough to eat!

What you need:
• *2 cups flour*

- ¾ cup water
- ½ cup salt
- Large mixing bowl
- Measuring cups
- Cutting board
- Rolling pin
- Christmas cookie cutters
- Drinking straw
- Baking sheet
- Acrylic paint
- Paintbrushes
- Ball of yarn or heavy string (cut into 6-inch pieces)

What you do:

1. Preheat the oven to 300°F.

2. Using your hands, mix together flour, water, and salt in the large bowl. Knead it well. You can add a little more water if the dough is too dry and is cracking, or you can add more flour if the dough seems too sticky. You'll want it so that you can roll it out easily.

3. Spread a little flour on the cutting

board, then place the dough on it.

4. Use the rolling pin to roll out the dough so that it's about a half inch thick.

5. Use the cookie cutters to cut shapes in the dough.

6. Then use the straw to poke a hole at the top of the shape so you'll be able to hang it.

7. Place the ornaments on the cookie sheet and bake in oven for one and a half hours.

8. Let them cool and dry (you can leave them out for a few days to completely dry).

9. Paint them using acrylic paints. Let the paint dry, then insert ribbon or string that's about 6 inches long through the hole. Tie a knot at one end so that you can hang it from the tree.

?

CHAPTER SEVEN

Getting-to-Know-You Games

Getting-to-know-you games offer something extra special: They help you
learn more about your friends while you're
having a good time. They're also great as
icebreakers — to play in situations where
not everyone knows one another so well.
Here are some favorites.

THE INTRODUCTION SONG

Here's a fast way to get a group of girls
who don't know one another on a first-
name basis! Sit cross-legged in a circle facing one another. Start the game by
slapping your palms on your thighs twice,
clapping twice, and then snapping one
hand at a time as you say your name. The

girl sitting to your right goes next by slapping her thighs, clapping her hands, snapping one hand, and saying your name, then snapping her other hand as she says her own name. The girl who goes next repeats the procedure, ending by snapping three times — to your name, the second girl's name, and finally her own name. Continue going around the entire circle.

If someone in the circle forgets a name, you have to start all over again. The game ends after each girl completes her turn correctly.

WHAT'S YOUR LINE?

Here's an idea that lets you share information about yourself and learn more about your friends.

To play the game, you'll need three-by-five-inch cards or small strips of paper, a pencil for each girl, and a basket, bowl, or hat to put the folded sheets of paper in.

Hand each girl a few strips of paper and

a pencil. Start the game by asking a question, such as:

- *What's your favorite food?*
- *What's your all-time favorite movie?*
- *If you could visit any place in the world, where would you go?*
- *What do you want to be when you grow up?*
- *What's your favorite item of clothing?*

Have each girl write her answer to the question on a strip of paper. (Hint: Disguise your writing.) Then have everyone fold their cards and place the answers in the basket. Shake the basket gently, and have each girl draw a card and open it. If she draws her own, she should put it back in and choose another.

One at a time, each girl reads the answer on the card she is holding. Go around the room and have everyone guess whose answer she has read. No one should admit which response is hers until everyone has guessed. Whoever guesses correctly gets a point.

Now let the next person in the group ask a question, and repeat the same procedure. Keep going until all the cards or strips of paper have been read. The girl who has the most points at the end of the game wins!

DO YOU KNOW YOUR NEIGHBOR?

In this game, start by having all the girls sit in a circle. Give each girl a sheet of paper and a pen or pencil. Someone asks a question (like those listed above for "What's Your Line?"). But instead of writing down *your* answers to the question, write down what you think the person sitting on your left would say.

Don't reveal any of your answers until each girl has asked a question. Once you've all asked questions, go around the circle and have each girl give her own answer to the question. Then ask her neighbor to read what she wrote and see how well she was able to guess. For every correct answer she has made about you, you both get a point! And for every time you correctly guessed what your other neighbor would say, you and she each get a point! After you've finished going through the questions, count your score. The person with the most points wins.

FEELINGS

Get ready to talk about your feelings. Before you begin playing this game, write the following words on small pieces of paper (one word per piece of paper):

Love
Hate
Sad
Happy
Fun
Boring
Crazy

Tired
Bad
Hurt
Angry
Frightened
Cold
Hot
Surprised
Proud

Fold each sheet of paper in half and place inside a basket or bowl. Then have all your friends get together and sit in a circle. Select a girl to go first. She draws a word from the basket, and then talks about a time when she felt that emotion. For instance, if she drew *proud*, she might talk about doing very well on a test. If she drew *hot*, she might tell everyone about a trip her family took to South America. After she finishes her turn, the girl sitting to her right takes a turn by drawing another emotion clue from the basket and saying her answer. The game is over after all of the emotion clues have been drawn.

CHAPTER EIGHT

Word Games

The best part about word games is that you can play them anytime or any-place, like while you're stuck in the car or waiting in a long line somewhere.

WOULD YOU RATHER . . .

The rules for this game are simple — the first girl starts the game by asking another girl a question that begins with "Would you rather . . ." For instance, your friend might ask you, "Would you rather have to stand up and sing 'My Country 'Tis of Thee' in front of the entire class or wear really dirty clothes to school every day for a week?" To make it even more fun, have the other girls first guess which answer they think you will choose. Then reveal your choice. You have to pick one answer or the other!

TWENTY QUESTIONS

To play twenty questions, first think of a person, place, animal, or object. Don't tell any of your friends what it is. It's their job to try to guess by asking no more than a total of twenty yes or no questions. (Yes or no questions can only be answered with a yes or no — in other words, no details!) After each girl asks you a question, she tries to guess what you're thinking of. The girl who guesses first wins and gets to think up the next clue. Since there are about a million persons, places, animals, and objects, here are some sample questions that can help narrow down the choices:

- *Is it a person?*
- *Is it an animal?*
- *Is it someone I know personally?*
- *Is it something I have in my house?*
- *Is it bigger than a lunchbox?*
- *Is it in this room?*

TELEPHONE

To play the game, everyone should sit or stand in a line. Then you need to come up with a silly phrase. It should be one really long sentence, like, "Mary went to the seashore to try and spot a gray whale, but all she saw were seven dolphins swimming alone in the deep blue ocean."

Whisper the phrase to the girl next to you. You can only say the phrase once! Then she has to whisper the same phrase, as well as she can remember it, to the next girl. Keep going around until all girls have heard the "rumor." The last one who hears it needs to say it aloud. Once she repeats it, say the line you started off with and see just how mixed up the phrase has become!

SECRET WORD

You only need to have one friend with you to take part in this game. Here's how it works: Come up with an oddball word —

one that people don't say all the time. The stranger, the better. Then see how long it takes you to get someone else to say it, without giving the word away! Say your friend comes up with the word *bumblebee*. You then go up to your mom and say things like, "I think I got stung," or, "I'd like to be something black and yellow for Halloween this year. Do you have any suggestions?" Your mom will probably look at you a little strangely, but that's okay — so long as you can get her to say *bumblebee* in a hurry! You have one minute total to get someone else to say your secret word. Let your friend count the time it takes, using a stopwatch or a watch with a second hand. Then it's your turn to come up with an equally odd word that your friend has to get someone else to say.

ALPHABET WORLD

Hope you've been doing your geography homework, because this game will put your knowledge of the world to the test. Select someone to go first. She has to come up with a city, state, country, or continent that begins with the letter A (like Asia or Amsterdam). The next girl then has to come up with one starting with the letter B (like Boston or Brazil). Keep going through the alphabet, leaving the letter X out of the game. (X is really hard. You can add it for an "Xtra" challenge). If someone gets stumped, she's out of the game. Keep going through the alphabet until everyone is out but one girl — the winner!

CELEBRITY CHAIN GAME

Do you know the names of tons of movie stars and celebrities? If so, you'll do very well at this game.

Here's how to play:

The person who is selected to go first says the name of someone famous . . . it can be anyone. Then it's up to the next person to come up with a celebrity whose name begins with the last letter of the first celebrity's name. For instance, if the first girl said, "Julia Roberts," then the next girl would have to come up with a famous person whose name begins with the letter S, like Sarah Michelle Gellar, and so on. . . . See who can keep going the longest without getting stumped.

CHAPTER NINE

Ideas that Make "Cents"

Are you looking for a way to earn a little extra spending money? Why not go into business with a friend? Here are some ideas that really make cents!

MAKE A LEMONADE STAND

There's nothing better than an ice-cold glass of homemade lemonade on a warm day. Maybe that's why lemonade stands have been around for ages! With a few ingredients and some supplies, you and your friends can create your own lemonade stand.

What you need:
- *A few pitchers*
- *Plastic or paper cups*

- *Folding table and chairs*
- *Banner paper or poster board and markers, to make your sign*
- *Cash box and a few dollars' in change (you can use a shoe box instead of a cash box)*
- *Lots of lemonade (see recipe below or prepare frozen lemonade from concentrate)*

What you do:

Prepare the lemonade before you set up outside. You'll also want to create signs to attract customers. Bright-colored poster board is great for signs that really stand out! Use dark, thick markers to write the word LEMONADE in large letters on the sign, and write the price so it's visible.

It's a good idea to set up your lemonade stand where people will see it — like at a Little League game or in front of a house on a busy street. Set up your table and chairs, and tape your sign to the table so others can see it. You're ready for business!

Be sure to have two or more people at the stand at any time, and have a grown-up nearby to help you if needed.

After you close down, divide the money between the participants. Make sure to pay back whoever paid for the supplies before you split your profits.

RECIPE: HOMEMADE LEMONADE

What you need:

- ◆ 12 lemons
- ◆ ½ cup sugar
- ◆ 8 cups cold water
- ◆ Ice cubes
- ◆ Cutting board
- ◆ Citrus juicer
- ◆ Small spoon
- ◆ Measuring cups
- ◆ Small bowl
- ◆ Long wooden spoon

◆ 2 large pitchers

What you do:

1. Have an adult cut the lemons in half for you.

2. Squeeze the juice out of each lemon using the citrus juicer.

3. Put the juice in a small bowl, and remove any seeds using a small spoon. Once you have squeezed six lemons, place the juice from them in one pitcher.

4. Squeeze the remaining lemons and place the juice in the second pitcher. Add ¼ cup of sugar to each pitcher of juice and stir well with the wooden spoon until blended.

5. Add 4 cups water to each pitcher, then fill with ice cubes.

6. Stir again, and add additional sugar if needed.

Makes about 20 cups of lemonade.

NOT JUST LEMONADE

A lemonade stand isn't the only stand you can create. Try one of these alternatives if lemonade doesn't suit your taste:

◆ **Bake Stand:** Sell brownies, cookies, and other homemade goodies

◆ **Fruit Punch Stand:** Make flavored drinks from a powdered mix

◆ **Homemade Popsicle Stand:** Fill a cup three-quarters full with punch, then place a piece of plastic wrap over the top. Punch a hole in the middle of the plastic wrap by inserting a Popsicle stick into the punch. Then freeze. Be sure to keep the Popsicles in a cooler containing ice so that they don't melt.

CAR WASH

Help keep the neighborhood cars clean by setting up a car wash. You'll need a paved area to wash the cars — like your driveway. You'll also need a bucket, sponges, a mild liquid soap, a hose that's hooked up, and lots of clean, dry towels.

Decide on a day and time that you and your friends will hold your car wash. Then design a flyer that you can post around the neighborhood. List the day and time of the car wash, the price, and the location. You might also want to come up with a clever line to help sell your services, like: "Does Your Car Need a Good Bath?" or "Want to Find Out What Color Your Car Really Is Under All That Dirt? Then Come to Our Car Wash."

On the day of the car wash, you can also put up a sign or banner at the place where you'll be washing the cars.

You might want to select a price per car between three dollars and five dollars. Ask your parents what professional car washes in the neighborhood charge, then come up with a price that's lower than that.

Prepare for the first car by hooking up the hose and filling a bucket with water and a little soap. In order to move quickly, it's a good idea to have each girl handle a different job — one girl can rinse the cars with water, another can use the soapy water and sponges to clean the car, and another can dry the car.

Car washing is hard work — so be sure to take breaks and drink lots of fluids while you're on the job!

DOG-WALKING SERVICE

Busy working people often don't have enough time to complete their day-to-day chores, like walking the dog. That's where you and your friends can help!

Create a flyer that promotes your dog-walking services, then distribute to neighbors that you know have pets. Leave your phone number on the flyer so that they can get in touch with you.

Arrange to walk dogs at a time that works for your schedules. Be sure that the dogs you agree to walk are well behaved! It's also much safer to walk one dog at a time — otherwise, the dogs may start fighting. Along with your friend or friends, walk the dog in a safe place during daylight hours. If it's hot out, be sure the dog gets plenty of water before and after the walk.

If you're an animal lover, dog-walking could be the perfect job for you! Even better, it offers you a chance to go on walks with your friends. And if things work out well, it's something you can do to earn money on a regular basis.

NEIGHBORLY NEWSLETTER

People love to hear about what's going on with other people they know. They also love to read about themselves! You and your friends can tap into their curiosity by creating a newsletter all about your neighborhood.

First you'll need to become junior reporters. Ask friends and neighbors what's new in their lives. Did someone just move in? Did someone just have a baby? Has someone done something special for the community? If neighbors have just returned from vacation, ask them all about the trip and take notes! You can also find out if someone is planning a garage sale, or if they are trying to sell something. Once you have a few juicy tidbits from your neighborhood, it's time for you and your pals to turn into editors and art designers!

Write a few of your favorite stories down. Then come up with other fun articles and features, like a joke or riddle, a word game, or ideas for fun things to do in your hometown. Then it's time to design the newsletter. Come up with a catchy name for it. You might want to include the name of your street or neighborhood as part of the name (like the *Elm Street*

Chatterbox or *Stone Lakes Reporter*). If you have access to a computer, use a newsletter program to create the story, or write the stories in a word-processing program using different sizes of type and different margin widths. Then you can print the stories, cut them out, and paste them down on a sheet or sheets of paper. You can even paste down a picture or photo, or use a computer scanner to place one in your newsletter. Make a small amount of copies at the grocery store or a copy center.

Once the newsletter is finished and printed, it's up to you and your friends to get out and sell it to neighbors. Decide on a price, like fifty cents, then hit the road together to spread the news!

CHORE SERVICE

Help out those people in the neighborhood who are either too busy or unable to do household chores. Here's a list of services you and your pals can offer:

- *Picking up leaves*
- *Taking out the garbage*
- *Sweeping porches*
- *Recycling*
- *Weeding or planting flowers*
- *Dog-washing*
- *Wrapping gifts during the holidays*
- *Watering lawns and plants*

Once you've come up with a list of chores you can handle, create an eye-catching flyer listing your names and phone numbers. Decide ahead of time how much you'll charge for each service. Then take it around to the neighbors. You'll hopefully soon hear from people who want to put you and your pals to work!

Friendship Fun Forever

Friends and fun go together hand in hand. So even after you've tried every idea in the book, chances are you won't run out of ways to have fun with your friends. As long as you have a great imagination (and every girl does!), you can create your own games, crafts, and activities.

But remember that not every minute you spend with your friends needs to be action-packed. The times you'll treasure most are often those spent just being together — talking, laughing, and sharing your stories and feelings. When you're with your friends, make every moment count, no matter what you're up to!